THE TASTE OF OUR TIME

Collection planned and directed by

ALBERT SKIRA

TEXT BY

JEAN LEYMARIE

Translated from the French by Stuart Gilbert

Picasso Drawings

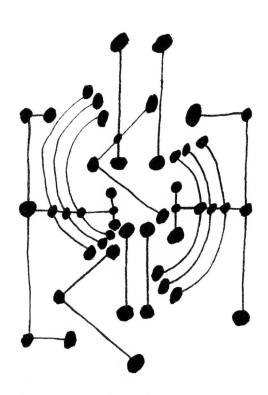

LIKE the greatest masters, Picasso is an all-round, universal artist and the creative unity of his genius makes itself felt in very different fields. In all the rich diversity of his creations, where each technique has its distinctive timbre and tone, line has everywhere and always played a leading part. Not, in terms of its classical function, as defining the natural shape of every form, but in its modern, empirical acceptation, as an essential concomitant of the act of seeing.

Picasso knew how to draw before he knew how to talk, but, as he himself has told us, there was nothing childish about even his first drawings. From the very start, his sharpness of observation was such that the correct movement of his hand followed automatically, without a moment's hesitation. As a schoolboy at Malaga in southern Spain, his birthplace, where every object stands out distinctly in the brilliant light, he amazed his playmates by tracing on the sand, in a single, continuous line, the exact form of a horse or bull he had seen on Sunday at the bullfight, and he brought off the same feat at home with scissors and paper under the admiring eyes of his sisters and girl cousins. At Corunna, in Galicia, where he went to study some years later, he disciplined his hand by copying, and amused himself drawing on his letters to his family in Andalusia sketches of local happenings that caught his eye. When he was thirteen his father, a drawing master, recognizing his exceptional talents and his wholehearted devotion to art, had the sense to realize there was nothing more he could teach the boy.

Henceforth he struggled ceaselessly to curb his virtuosity, and to transform the facility which came to him so naturally into an instrument for rendering visual experience with complete fidelity. For him conception and execution were inseparable. This was because his drawing answered less to any aesthetic preoccupation than to a vital urge which found fulfilment in sudden flashes of inspiration.

This explains why it is impossible to speak of any evolution, in the accepted sense of the term, in the art of Picasso; what we find in it is, rather, a sequence of instinctive responses to personal and social conditions of the moment.

Except during the period when he was working out the theory of Cubism or engaged on large-scale paintings or sculptures, Picasso's graphic work proceeded by and large, in all its various forms, on completely independent lines. While as regards style and inspiration it linked up with his painting, it shows divergencies and developments peculiar to itself. Also we find that sometimes in whole periods when he tended to employ a single color, and in such large monochrome works as *The Milliner's Workroom* (1926), *Guernica* (1937), the two variants of *The Kitchen* (1948) and the first version of *Las Meninas* (1957), the major role is assigned to drawing. Conversely, many pastels and gouaches, technically included among the drawings, have the same rich texture, the same lavish color as the oil paintings.

*

This zest for drawing predominated in the hectic years the young artist spent in Barcelona, where a cultural revival was in progress, in the company of the Bohemian, anarchist-minded avant-garde. This period was marked by surprise visits to Madrid and Paris. A phase of desperate struggles and privations, it was rich for him in human contacts and new visual discoveries, and in it he accumulated a wealth of potentialities for the future. The illustrations he published in modernist reviews—tavern and street scenes, portraits and self-portraits—demonstrate, beneath the then fashionable stylizations of Art Nouveau, a keen insight into situations and character, and a singular dexterity, concise, often touched with irony, in the handling of form.

Gradually this ruthless analysis of minds and manners yielded to a gentler mood; unflinching naturalism to poetic idealization. Thus began that early, stylistically uniform phase known as the Blue Period (1901-1904) in virtue of the prevailing night-blue tone of these pictures of gaunt, poverty-stricken humanity. Though influenced by El Greco, the vogue for whom was in full stride, and by the idioms of Gothic and Mannerist art, Picasso now developed that powerfully expressive line peculiar to himself which has persisted throughout his long career.

After he came to live in Paris (April 1904) his liaison with Fernande Olivier, contacts with poets and their championship of his art led him to take a happier view of life; the melancholy of the Blue Period gave place to a nostalgic grace. His strolling acrobats (inspiration of one of Rilke's Duino elegies) and the pensive harlequins of the Rose Period invited the use of a medium capable of subtler, more eloquent effects—watercolor, pastel, gouache—crisscrossed by nervous penstrokes tersely defining the contours of figures. In the most representative drawings of this period all three techniques are combined. It was now that he made a series of watercolors enhanced with gouache, remarkable for their spontaneity and sensitivity, intended to serve as preliminary studies for three large compositions on the theme of *Saltimbanques* (circus folk) that Picasso planned to paint in 1905; the only one of them brought to completion is in the National Gallery, Washington. The theme of motherhood recurs, but he treats it now with a tenderness and delicate emotion having nothing of the mood of social protest that had engloomed the Blue Period.

Between his trip to Holland in June 1905 and his stay at Gosol (Spanish Pyrenees) the following summer Picasso went through a first phase of serene and smiling classicism. This was partly due to outside influences: those of Gauguin and Renoir, and to an active interest in antique sculpture; but also and above all to his personal evolution, a shift away from phantoms of the imagination towards objective, simplified, harmonious forms. The key work of this period of classical purity was to be a large composition, *The Watering Place*, showing naked young men riding and leading horses to drink at a pond; some admirable preliminary studies for this major work exist.

The exhibition of pre-Romanesque Iberian sculpture at the Louvre in early 1906 came as a revelation. Followed by three months of solitude and meditation in a remote Catalan mountain village, it led to a sudden, drastic change in his art. He replaced classical form and its terse, clear-cut contours by a primitive, not to say archaizing style, all in compact volumes. Blank, masklike faces surmount massive bodies with ponderous limbs; individuality is submerged in physical plenitude, the man himself withdrawn into an inner world.

In some group sketches executed in watercolor or pastel, and in certain notations of details made in the spring of 1907, we find intimations of the tremendous dynamism and the complex forces that culminated in the epoch-making *Demoiselles d'Avignon*. This hallucinating composition, with its disconcerting breaks of structural continuity, gave a new, dramatic impetus to modern art by radically destroying the illusionist tradition and shifting the center of gravity to the picture itself and the creative tension pervading it. All the sentimental or illustrative values of the past were disintegrated, diffused in waves of energy binding figures to the ground, volumes to space.

This drastic innovation pointed the way to Cubism and the new, non-perspectival method of representing volumes wholly on a flat surface. In the course of execution a unity developed between the multiform structure of objects and figures and the architectonic rhythm of the picture as an organic whole. Throughout the analytic phase of Cubism, which to begin with aimed at rendering form at the expense, for the time being, of color (also excluded from the drawings, almost always in lead pencil or charcoal), this linear discipline was an indispensable aid to the gradual mastery of the pictorial content and perfect sureness of hand. Drawing also played a signal part in the new technique of *papiers collés*, that remarkable invention of the autumn of 1912 which led up to Synthetic Cubism, the restoration of color and the creation of what was nothing short of a new metaphorical and conceptual art language.

Next, Picasso reverted to watercolor and gouache, washes of bright tints applied to constructs of flat, superimposed planes. In 1914, while exploring and exploiting the possibilities of this new allusive method, almost abstract in its schematization, he also took to pencilling meticulously realistic still lifes. In the following year, as if to prove that, despite the distracting influences of the war, he "could still draw like everybody else," he made the famous pencil portraits of Vollard and Max Jacob, in which every detail is recorded with minute precision. These inaugurated an amazing series of portraits, in which Picasso's mastery of line advanced from strength to strength, culminating in 1920 in the likenesses of the three musicians, Erik Satie, Igor Stravinsky and Manuel de Falla, in which all the essential work is done by the contour alone.

This usage of conflicting styles caused much surprise. Some saw in it the sign of a versatile temperament unable to decide between an innate urge to revolutionary experiments and deference to tradition. The truth lies elsewhere. There was no real conflict or antinomy; simply a following of two parallel paths, one of them conventional only in appearance. For though the naturalistic portraits cannot fail to remind us of Ingres, in view of their insistence on technique and character-revealing traits, their somewhat Cézannesque spatial organization incorporates many of the new visual discoveries of Cubism.

In this age of aesthetic relativity when all the arts of the past were becoming contemporary again, and each style was seen to be justifiable on its own terms, and none could claim exclusive merit, Picasso felt free to choose according to the inspiration of the moment and the nature of the subject, the mode of expression best suited to it. As a result of this shift in the historical perspective, it was possible for an artist to ring the changes on several types of art hitherto thought incompatible. But this could be completely achieved, without running the risk of eclecticism or incoherence, only by an artist having a temperament as richly endowed as Picasso's, capable of remaining true to itself and safeguarding its intrinsic coherence in an infinite diversity of forms.

The significant dualism we first find in his graphic art was transmitted to his paintings and became generalized after his trip to Rome in 1917. Synthetic Cubism, which achieved so magnificent a flowering in his renderings of subjects drawn from the Commedia dell'Arte and in elaborate still lifes, coexisted for several years with a second, thoroughly classical, monumental type of painting—a trend particularly evident in the domain of graphic art. Several of Picasso's drawings of this period gravitate around such major, finely balanced and co-ordinated compositions as *Women at the Fountain* (1921) and *The Pipes of Pan* (1923), but many of the other drawings are quite independent works. Treated in an heroic or lyrical mode they have a fluent grace, a perfection of form, ranking them beside the masterworks of the Renaissance and Antiquity. Picasso's yearly visits to the seaside, his contacts with the Russian ballet and his marriage to one of the stars of Diaghilev's troupe stimulated his pagan cult of the human body, leading motif of classical art and pretext for so many plastic or graphic experiments. This calm, classicizing figure style, violently interrupted in his paintings after 1925, lasted much longer in his drawings and prints, culminating magnificently in the large cycles of etchings made for Ovid's *Metamorphoses* (1931) and *The Sculptor's Studio* (1933).

This brilliant interlude, classical and realistic, answering both to the artist's personal inclinations and to the aesthetic climate of the time, divides Picasso's graphic work into two essential phases. The first, the phase of Cubism, was characterized by an investigation of form leading to a clarification and mastery of pictorial structure and an almost constant use of "naked" instruments—pen, pencil, charcoal—

making clear-cut, incisive lines. Meanwhile the techniques of color—pastel, gouache, watercolor—were resorted to only intermittently, from 1907 to 1909, 1914 to 1923.

But after 1930, and still more markedly after 1933, when Picasso's trip to Spain had revived his interest in subjects drawn from bullfights and in the expression of his personal feelings, there came a phase that can be properly described as autobiographical (though there were no self-portraits, only allegorical equivalents). In this period he took to larger formats, thematic developments in series, and a more emphatic, lavish use—like "writing with the brush"—of washes of Indian ink, dappled with broken gleams, enlivened with expressive color. The instinctual drive of the emotions, their joys and pains, their conflicts, the parts they play, sensuous or tragic, in the human situation, is given free rein, if sometimes veiled by touches of humor or glossed by a mythological allusion. This obsession with mythological subjects (much more frequent in the drawings than in the paintings, and tending to recur in cycles) often coincides with the first appearance of new images of "love": *Minotaur* in 1933, *Naiads and Fauns* in 1946, *Bacchanals* in 1955. Picasso shares with Rembrandt with whom, on his most expressive plane, he has affinities, the knack of directly imparting to the most personal experiences a universal application, and of sublimating to the level of myth the incidents of daily life on which he draws persistently.

Excluded from his painting, surrealist influence can be seen in some of the drawings made in the summer of 1933. A long series of violently emotive figurations consists of preludes and postscripts to that transcendent monochrome painting, *Guernica* (1937). The dislocated figure pieces of 1938 are patterned with curious spider-web arabesques, suggestive of a mixed Andalusian-Moorish descent; indeed they often give an impression of an unresolved struggle between Arab calligraphy and Mediterranean anthropomorphism. This is what Apollinaire had in mind when he spoke of Picasso as being "more Latin in his thinking, more Arab in his rhythm."

Stemming one would say from time immemorial —such is its majestic simplicity—the large sculpture *Man with a Lamb*, though executed in a single day at the darkest hour of the war, was the end-product of months of preparation, evidenced by a host of sketches, each of independent merit. The same weight of stark humanity finds concrete expression in the monumental pencil drawing *Woman washing her Feet* (May 1944). This figure with its characteristic gesture recurs almost as often in Picasso's work as that of the sleeping woman with a seated man beside her. The watercolor copy of Poussin's *Bacchanal* made at the end of August 1944, just after the Liberation of Paris, was the thematic and stylistic starting point of the gay cycle deployed on the walls of the Château Grimaldi at Antibes. Picasso's stay at Vallauris, on the Riviera, gave birth to an amazing sequence of 180 drawings made in the winter of 1953-1954, a merciless critique of academic art, indeed of all forms of art that are not rooted in life itself. At Cannes, where once again a happy life began for him, he made the joyous portraits of Jacqueline, a cycle of studio interiors, and that magnificent last series of aquatints of bullfights.

At several moments of his life, for various reasons —in 1935, 1953 and 1966—Picasso ceased painting, but he never seems to have ceased drawing; drawing is to him the breath of life. Since moving to a new house at Mougins (summer 1961), he has shown a preference for color crayons, due no doubt to the possibilities they give for blending linear and pictorial techniques. Sometimes he concentrates on isolated heads, independently of any anecdotal context and viewed in close-up; but sometimes, too, he indulges the verve of a born narrator telling his tale in images. His technical proficiency and his insight into the human predicament have reached a point where all trace of "style" disappears in the compelling impact of the graphic image.

PICASSO DRAWINGS

ENHANCED with washes of watercolor, this pen and ink drawing, made in Paris in 1904, soon after Picasso had moved into the Bateau Lavoir in Montmartre, is a touching piece of autobiography. For there can be no doubt that the figure of the man seen in side view between the table and the bed, with a lock of hair falling across his forehead, a slim hand cupping an aggressive chin, and contemplating pensively the girl quietly sleeping, all passion spent, is a self-portrait. Everything in his look and attitude tells of tenacity of purpose and intense concentration. The gaze of the artist, we feel, is only half directed to the young grace of his companion; it seems also to be turned inward, as if he were trying to plumb the mystery of every human destiny, his own in particular. Art, for him, is an expression of his inmost life, the truth that is in him.

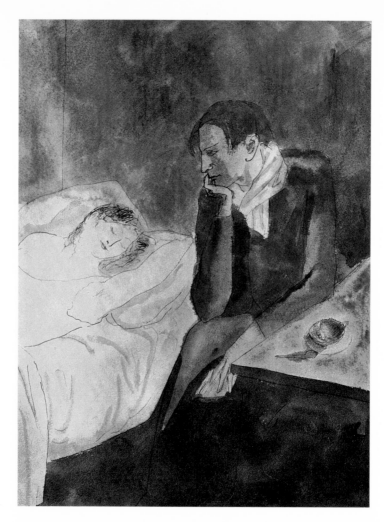

MEDITATION, 1904.

A MOTHER HOLDING A CHILD, 1904.

THIS pencil sketch, also dating to 1904, was a preliminary study for several large gouaches and pastels. The extreme elegance of the line, reminiscent of the best examples of Late Gothic or Mannerist art, is invested with an expressive pathos that is wholly original. The design of the long, sinuous hand is repeated four times on the sheet; and there is also a repetition of the graceful inclination of the mother's bust as she bends over her child.

The next watercolor, patterned with lively, syncopated penstrokes, shows a group of circus folk —one of Picasso's favorite subjects in his Rose Period—taking the air in front of their tent, with a white horse and an upright ladder in the background. This was a sketch for one of three big compositions on the "Bateleurs" (mountebanks) theme which he planned to paint in 1905; only one of them—the one celebrated by Rilke in the fifth of his Duino elegies— was brought to completion. It is now in the National Gallery, Washington.

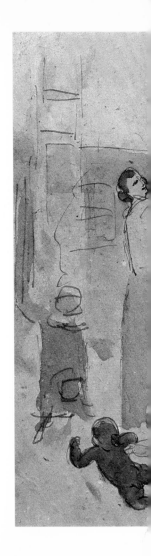

CIRCUS FAMILY, 1905.

3

SHEET WITH STUDIES FOR THE SELF-PORTRAIT OF 1906.

PICASSO made a great number of self-portraits, some of them paintings but mostly drawings, in the years preceding Cubism. This sheet of studies, some of the face alone rendered with a masklike fixity, others of the whole bust showing the arms in movement, links up with the *Self-Portrait with Palette* (Philadelphia Museum of Art), dating to the fall of 1906, in which exact resemblance is transcended by a kind of visionary objectivity.

His discovery of pre-Romanesque Iberian sculpture and his stay at Gosol, a lonely village in the high valley of Andorra, led to what was nothing short of a thorough change of heart, a transmutation of the emotive values dominant in his previous work into purely plastic values. The two charcoal drawings he made in that crucial year (1906)—a female nude and a group of two women, one seated and one standing—illustrate this abrupt transition from *classical* form, all in fine-spun contours, to *primitive* form, squat and ponderous.

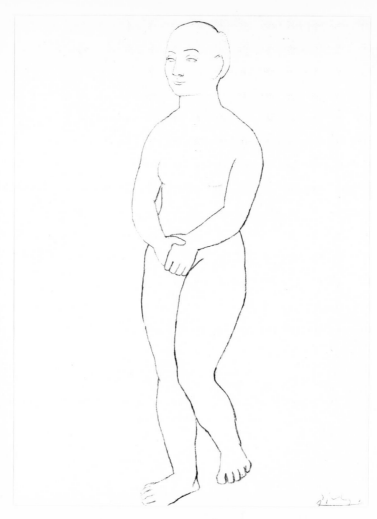

NUDE, 1906.

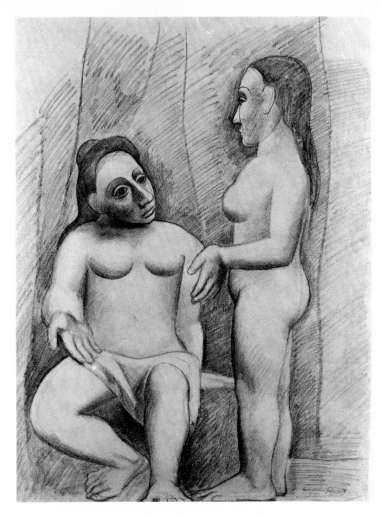

WOMAN SEATED AND WOMAN STANDING, 1906.

STUDY FOR "LES DEMOISELLES D'AVIGNON," 1907.

BESIDES numerous studies of separate details, there exist several composition sketches in various techniques for that extraordinary picture, *Les Demoiselles d'Avignon* (1907), which marked a turning point in the artist's career and also, beyond all doubt, in the art of the whole century. This study in pencil and pastel shows one of the earliest stages of the composition, then given a symmetrical arrangement centering on a seated sailor. A student carrying a skull, *memento mori*, enters the room, lifting a curtain as he steps forward while, surrounded by flowers and fruit, the sailor is enjoying the uninhibited display of the ladies of the brothel. In the final version the two male figures, the vase of flowers and the *memento mori* allegory have disappeared. Only the figures of the five naked women, stylistically discrepant and blocked out with stark directness, create the all-over tension of the space into which they are incorporated.

THIS forceful pen and ink sketch, all in jagged streaks and hatchings (inspired by flat African masks), belongs to the early, so-called Negro phase of Cubism. It dates to 1908 and the monumental picture of the same subject, *Friendship*, is now in the Hermitage Museum, Leningrad.

The nudes on the following pages, drawn in charcoal, illustrate the development and orientation of Analytic Cubism: first, structuration of the volumes of the body as a whole in compact, simply stated masses; then its internal break-up into a complex of facets facing in different directions. In the spring of 1910, the treatment of the theme becomes "hermetic"; the human form is disintegrated and crystallized in an elaborate trellis-work of angles and open arcs.

FRIENDSHIP, 1908.

KNEELING FIGURE, 1908.

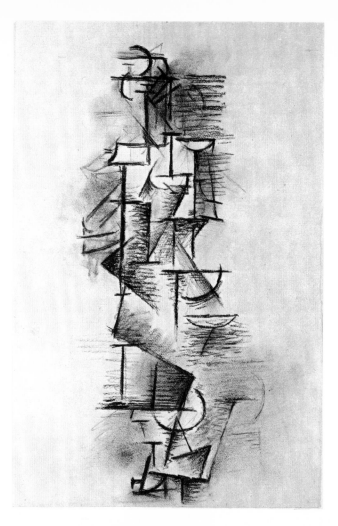

FEMALE NUDE, 1910.

SUGAR BOWL AND FAN, 1910.

THOUGH during this period Picasso was chiefly interested in the human figure, he sometimes tried his hand at the still life, a theme in which Braque, with whom he was in close and constant contact, was specializing. If, from 1909 to 1912, the fan or a fanlike pattern recurs so often in his work, this is because the way it opens out matches so aptly the articulation of the "new space" he has in mind. However, he very rarely has recourse to watercolor in this phase of tension and austerity.

In the next two drawings the volumetric nucleus of the head, while losing nothing of its individuality and distinctive traits, is resolved into a system of superimposed, delicately modulated planes. The geometric rigor of the composition does not preclude a touch of humor in the pipe-smoker's moustache.

ALGERIAN WOMAN, 1910.

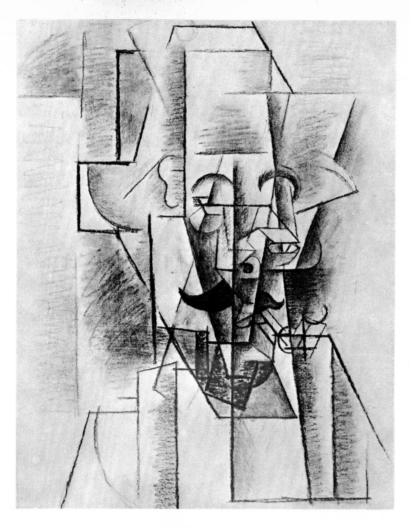

MAN WITH A PIPE, 1912.

STILL LIFE WITH BISCUITS, 1914.

After the first experiments with *papiers collés* in the fall of 1912, the technique of Cubism was reversed: from analytic it became synthetic. Picasso was quick to see the possibilities of this new conceptual language and during his summer stay at Avignon in 1914 inserted a rich diversity of decorative elements or (as in this pencil drawing) unexpected illusionist effects within the planimetric pictorial design. The different tactile values of the objects—the goffered corrugations of the biscuits, the texture of the paper, the smooth gloss of the plate, the veining of the wooden table—are rendered with surprising precision. Also in 1914 and 1915 he produced a large number of seated figures, often of a man holding a pipe or a musician with his instrument. Two finely conceived and executed drawings of this type are shown on the following pages.

MAN WITH A GUITAR, ABOUT 1914.

SEATED MAN WITH A PIPE, 1915.

PORTRAIT OF AMBROISE VOLLARD, 1915.

IF we study them attentively we find there is no real
cleavage in the handling of space, the organization
of the planes or even in the model's pose, between
the *Seated Man with Pipe*—despite its boldly synthetic
configuration—and the contemporary, meticulously
lifelike portrait of Vollard seated with his legs
crossed. Though down to the least detail the figure
itself is modeled on purely traditional lines, the
spatial organization is frankly revolutionary. The
Vollard portrait, made in August 1915, was hailed
as a masterpiece, such was its technical perfection,
but it shocked the orthodox disciples of Cubism,
who saw in it an apostasy. It was the starting point
of a whole series of pencil portraits, in an Ingresque
vein, two of which, made in 1920, we reproduce:
those of the composers Erik Satie and Igor Stravinsky with whom Picasso collaborated when he
was working for Diaghilev's Russian Ballet.

24-5-20.

PORTRAIT OF IGOR STRAVINSKY, 1920.

PORTRAIT OF ERIK SATIE, 1920.

THE BATHERS, 1918.

THIS elaborate, exquisitely designed composition has the purity of line of a Greek vase painting and the grace of a Botticelli, but its rhythmic vitality is all Picasso's. Made at Biarritz in the summer of 1918, *The Bathers* groups fifteen figures of nude women on the seashore in a wonderful variety of attitudes. Three motifs already used, or subsequently to be used, appear in it: a woman combing her hair, girls racing along a beach, the pair formed by a seated or squatting figure beside a reclining one.

Next summer, at Saint-Raphaël on the Riviera, Greek elegance gives place to robustness. The remarkable gouache of *Sleeping Peasants* inaugurates Picasso's so-called "colossal" figure style. Reminiscences of Rubens, Boucher, Millet and Ingres (in his late period) and of a harvesting scene recorded in a group of sketches enter into this grandiose composition like an open-air bas-relief instinct with warm, sensual humanity.

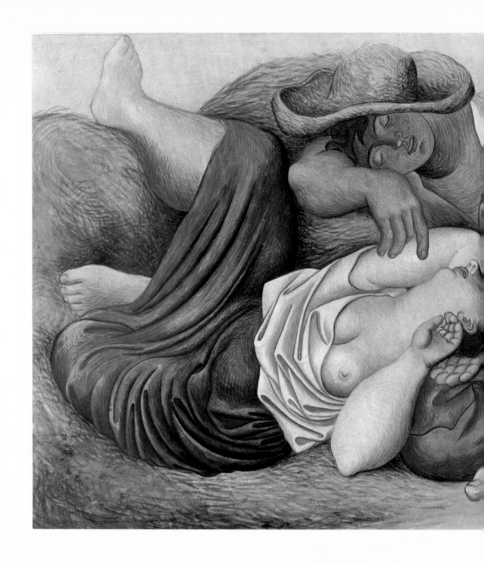

SLEEPING PEASANTS, 1919.

NESSUS AND DEIANIRA, 1920.

Picasso's neo-classical style, inaugurated in 1918 by *The Bathers*, combining bold foreshortenings and distortions with a meticulous linear perfection, reaches its culmination in *Nessus and Deianira*. At Juan-les-Pins in the summer of 1920 he came under the spell of the Mediterranean world and the ancient myths born on its sun-bathed shores. In eleven days (September 11-22) he made six pencil or silverpoint drawings, witty, grave or poetic, of the attempted rape of Deianira, wife of Hercules, by the centaur Nessus.

Now and in the succeeding summers when he roamed the Riviera beaches, dappled with the forms of scantily clad women, he rang the changes, with unfaltering ease and pagan delight, on the graceful, ever-changing arabesque of a woman's body, outstretched or standing, flooded with limpid light. Two lines drawn across the white sheet suffice to conjure up the luminous expanse of sea, sky and sand.

RECLINING BATHER, 1920.

NUDE, ABOUT 1925.

SLEEPING FEMALE NUDE AND SEATED MALE NUDE, 1931.

THE classicizing vein, serene and naturalistic, which Picasso discarded in his painting in 1925, lasted many years longer in his graphic art, as is evident from this admirable drawing of 1931. It would seem that this theme of two nude figures, one asleep, the other watching over the sleeper, had a special fascination for the artist, for it frequently recurs in his work under various forms. Sometimes, as here, it is the woman who is sleeping, an arm outstretched above her head so as to bring out the curves of the naked bust. Sometimes, as in the wash drawings of 1942, the situation is reversed: it is the woman who gazes intently at a sleeping man. In those of 1947, where both personages are women, the one awake is crouching forward, her eyes fixed on her companion.

THE only drawings of his which Picasso admits to be directly surrealistic in conception are those he made at Cannes in the summer of 1933. The best known of them, here reproduced, representing two figures on the beach, is made up of assorted odds and ends: broken-down articles of furniture, a tree-trunk, bits of statues, and studio bric-à-brac, not omitting a mirror and a glove. Are we to see in this new departure a reflection of the troubles of his married life, the threatened break-up of his home?

Yet only a week before he made this macabre drawing, and in a very different mood, of classical serenity, he had painted that superb gouache of a sculptor gazing at his statue, in which he reverted to the theme of one of the famous etchings he had made for Vollard in the spring of the same year. Here the statue, impervious to time, proudly confronts the perishable flesh-and-blood body of its naked, bearded, faunesque maker.

TWO FIGURES ON THE BEACH, 1933.

THE SCULPTOR AND HIS STATUE, 1933.   ___

Born in Philadelphia in 1890, Man Ray, after pioneering work with groups of vanguard American artists and meeting Marcel Duchamp in New York at the Armory Show (1913), moved to Paris in 1921. There he took part in the Dada and Surrealist movements as painter, photographer and film producer. Though the technique of this portrait differs completely from the strictly linear style of the earlier ones, the likeness is no less convincing. Man Ray has described, in his *Self Portrait* (1963), the way Picasso went about it. "I came to sit for him in a room without any heat—it was in January—and I kept my overcoat on. He squatted down on a small stool with a quart bottle of ink on the floor beside him, regardless of the blackening of his fingers, he began scratching the paper... He put a finger to his tongue and rubbed his drawing with it, repeating the operation. Presently his fingers, lips and tongue were black with ink."

PORTRAIT OF MAN RAY, 1934.

MINOTAUR, 1933.

THAT fabled Cretan monster, the Minotaur, half bull, half man, made a first sensational appearance in Picasso's art in 1933; it was to have a copious progeny in later years. This composition in Indian ink, dated Boisgeloup, June 28, is one of many studies for a sequence of etchings and drawings made by him that year. The brutal savaging of the woman and the bull-headed man's massive grip of his hapless victim are expressed with a plastic vehemence, a sensual brio almost unparalleled in art, even in the art of Rubens, and the sinewy line of the contours is enriched by baroque undulations of the wash.

In 1935 Picasso became the father of a child, whose mother could not share his home. In two Indian ink drawings he made in the following year (April 1936), remarkable for their dramatic handling of light, the family life centering on the little girl is presented in the guise of a mythological scene.

YOUNG FAUN, WOMAN AND CHILD, 1936.

FAMILY GROUP, 1936.

THE ritual animal of Spain, whose mythical ante-cedent is the Minotaur, figures prominently in *Guernica*, along with the horse, its associate and victim in the bullring. It is common knowledge that this stupendous composition, first exhibited at the Paris World's Fair of 1937, owes its name and moti-vation to the small Spanish town in the province of Biscay bombed by Nazi planes in broad daylight and without any military justification on April 28, 1937. Working at high pressure, Picasso made a number of preparatory studies, beginning May 1. He decided on the general layout on May 11 when he set to reworking each individual element so as to give it the utmost forcefulness and density. So it was that on May 20 he made this pencil drawing which, with a pattern of strongly expressive contrasting curves, figured forth this sinister bull's head, eerily resembling a bloated, malignant human face.

STUDY FOR "GUERNICA," 1937.

WE find an aftermath of the paroxysmal violence of *Guernica* in a series of heads of weeping women, painted, etched or drawn between the end of June and the end of October in the same year. Unlike *Guernica*, which was deliberately monochrome, but for the same expressive purpose, colors are now employed, sometimes harshly strident, sometimes, as here, in cold, lugubrious tones. Though the sharply angular, horse-like head, draped with a Spanish headdress, is shown in side view, both of the protruding eyes are visible, with two streams of tears trickling down the cheeks. This face is a speaking image of despair, and yet we can sense the model's distinction—finely shaped hands, slender neck—and there is a poignant beauty in the woman's gesture as she thrusts the handkerchief between her lips to still her cries.

WEEPING WOMAN (AFTER "GUERNICA"), 1937.

SEATED WOMAN, 1938.

PARTICULARLY in favor in the synthetic phase of Cubism, the seated figure has always been one of the central themes of Picasso's art. More especially, the figure of a woman sitting in an armchair recurs with a remarkable persistency in the period 1933-1949. This drawing bears the date September 8, 1938 and shows a naked woman sitting in front of her mirror, putting on a necklace with two rows of beads (another, almost identical version was made on the same day). She has the expressionistic face with a horse-like nose so often found in the works subsequent to *Guernica*. This decorative, geometrical calligraphy, reminiscent of basketry or chair caning and on occasion of the radiating pattern of spider's webs, characterizes most of the paintings and drawings of 1938.

THE CHAIR, 1942.

DURING the enforced seclusion of the war and the Occupation, Picasso turned his attention to domestic objects. The plain wooden chair, ennobled in a famous painting by Van Gogh, is rendered with no less expressive force but in a different language —a cursive linear scheme, with telling contrasts of light and shade.

This was also one of the periods when he devoted much of his time to sculpture, the major work of the war years being the *Man with a Lamb*, a large, free-standing statue whose origins and gradual elaboration can be traced in about a hundred preliminary sketches made between July 1942 and August 1943. The one reproduced on the next page is dated August 26, 1942. Beside the vigorously delineated shepherd, a man of ripe age, holding the lamb (this was the version finally adopted in the sculpture), stands another figure, a younger man, also with a lamb in his arms. The same handsome adolescent with a grave, strongly characterized face, who made his first appearance in this sequence of preparatory sketches, reappears in four independent wash drawings made in August 1944.

STUDIES FOR THE "MAN WITH A LAMB," 1942.

HEAD OF A BOY, 1944.

WOMAN WASHING HER FEET, 1944.

IN this monumental nude all illusionist conventions and all the traditional co-ordinates formed by straight lines defining the picture space are absent. It is self-contained in a curved space, and its tactile and dynamic effects certainly owe something to Degas, who had a special liking for subjects of this type. Picasso makes us sense, in terms of muscular convolutions and a simultaneous presentation of all its aspects, the movement of a human body engaged in a specific activity. The posture of a woman stooping to pick up her child, to gather flowers or, as here, to wash her feet had often figured in his earlier works. It was given fullest expression in the course of 1944, in a series of pencil studies made in May and another of ink wash sketches in July. Later this characteristic figure was integrated into group compositions, paintings as well as drawings.

IN September 1946 Picasso settled in the Château Grimaldi at Antibes and with an almost juvenile enthusiasm launched into the series of pastoral-mythological compositions now preserved in the castle museum and usually described, after the original Greek name of the town, as the Antipolis series. The largest of these pictures is *Joie de Vivre*, of which this watercolor is a preliminary version, plotted out in terms of a geometrical network of triangles, curves and circles. It, too, was the outcome of a series of earlier, more naturalistic drawings. The full-breasted maenad in the center, dancing and holding a tambourine over her head, derives from Poussin's *Bacchanal*, of which Picasso made a free copy in August 1944, just after the Liberation. The faun on the left, who in other studies is shown carrying a lamb or a goat and leaping into the air, is here turning a somersault, while his sprightly companion on the right plays the flute.

THE FLUTE PLAYER, 1946.

25.11.49.

VILLA LA GALLOISE AT VALLAURIS, 1949.

IT was in this small, banal, ramshackle villa, "La Galloise," that Picasso, never much concerned with the creature comforts of his home and its surroundings, lived from 1948 to 1954. (For his work he had studios in the neighboring village of Vallauris.) Situated on a hillside, La Galloise has, like many other houses in this part of France, a little garden, a terrace shaded by mulberry-trees and gets its water from a small nearby pond. This drawing is dated November 25, 1949; even in early winter Mediterranean trees and shrubs still keep their leaves. Landscape motifs are rare in Picasso's essentially humanistic art; on the few occasions when he uses them they are always accurately depicted and usually have a direct connection with his life and activities.

PICASSO drew and painted many portraits of his four children, Paulo, Maia, Claude and Paloma, in their tender years. Paloma, the youngest, was born in April 1949, at the time when pictures of a dove (*paloma* in Spanish), after which she was named, were being used all over the world as propaganda in the cause of peace. Her father was enchanted by her big, black, wide-open eyes, her animal spirits, her large round head with chubby cheeks, her plump little hands clasping a doll. In this drawing, on which Picasso worked for ten days (December 23, 1952 to January 3, 1953, as recorded in the upper righthand corner), the child's face, seen in close-up, is given an almost startling relief. The supple, widely ramifying line (in Indian ink) explores even the minutest crannies and recesses of the face, bringing out with clear-cut precision its expressive traits and volumes. To the same period belong other portraits, drawn, painted or lithographed, of the same model.

PORTRAIT OF PALOMA, 1953.

Between November 28, 1953, and February 3, 1954, Picasso made a brilliantly original series of a hundred and eighty drawings, some enhanced with ink wash. One of the peaks of his graphic work, it was also a revelation of the acuity of his insight into the human situation—his own in particular. Here the contrast, pathetic yet absurd, between an aged painter pedantically intent on his task and a young model flaunting her sensual charms with careless nonchalance, is exploited with irony and understanding. Some of the drawings of this series also relate to circus life, which is treated in the same spirit of light-hearted mockery—or disillusionment. Sometimes the model leaves the group, to frolic with a winged, masked cupid. A final sequence includes a magnificent, exceptionally elaborate water-color of a girl wearing a hat—she had already appeared sporadically in previous episodes; here she is teasing a monkey, holding up an apple out of its reach, watched by a jocund clown or satyr.

STUDIO SCENE, 1953.

THE STUDIO (MODELS), 1954.

NUDE WOMAN AND MASKED CUPID, 1954.

GIRL WITH A MONKEY, 1954.

21.10.55.

PORTRAIT OF JACQUELINE, 1955.

92

JACQUELINE ROQUE (now Madame Picasso), who first entered the artist's life in 1954, has been the inspiration of a long, unbroken series of portraits, in every possible technique, celebrating her grave beauty, long dark hair, finely molded features and gracious charm. It was assuredly her striking resemblance to one of the women in Delacroix's masterpiece, *Women of Algiers*, that suggested the series of fifteen variations on this theme that Picasso painted in Paris in the winter of 1954-1955. In some of the preliminary drawings the identification or substitution is unmistakable. Jacqueline and Picasso set up house in a 1900-style villa called La Californie, just above Cannes, and promptly transformed a wing of the large living-room into a studio, soon cluttered up with all the objects appropriate to an artist's work-room. It has high bay windows giving on the palm trees in the garden and it provided Picasso for some months with the theme of a cycle of magnificent drawings and paintings.

WOMEN OF ALGIERS, 1954.

THE STUDIO IN VILLA LA CALIFORNIE AT CANNES, 1955.

His move to the south of France in 1948 and the possibility of attending the bullfights that took place in Provence revived Picasso's innate taste for this typically Spanish theme. It was chiefly in ceramics and drawings that he gave rein to it. Perhaps the most brilliant achievements in this field were the aquatints made to illustrate the bullfighter's classic manual, published in 1796, by the famous matador Pepe Illo. Directly connected with this work and treated in the same style, which might be accurately described as "tachiste," is a remarkable series of wash drawings evoking deftly and concisely the successive phases of a bullfight. In recent years Picasso has shown a marked predilection for the technique of color crayons.

BULLFIGHT, 1957.

BATHSHEBA, 1963.   —